D1543614

As a Boy

Plan International

Second Story Press

Zimbabwe

Indonesia

Zambia

Bangladesh

Guatemala

Nepal

Boy or girl?

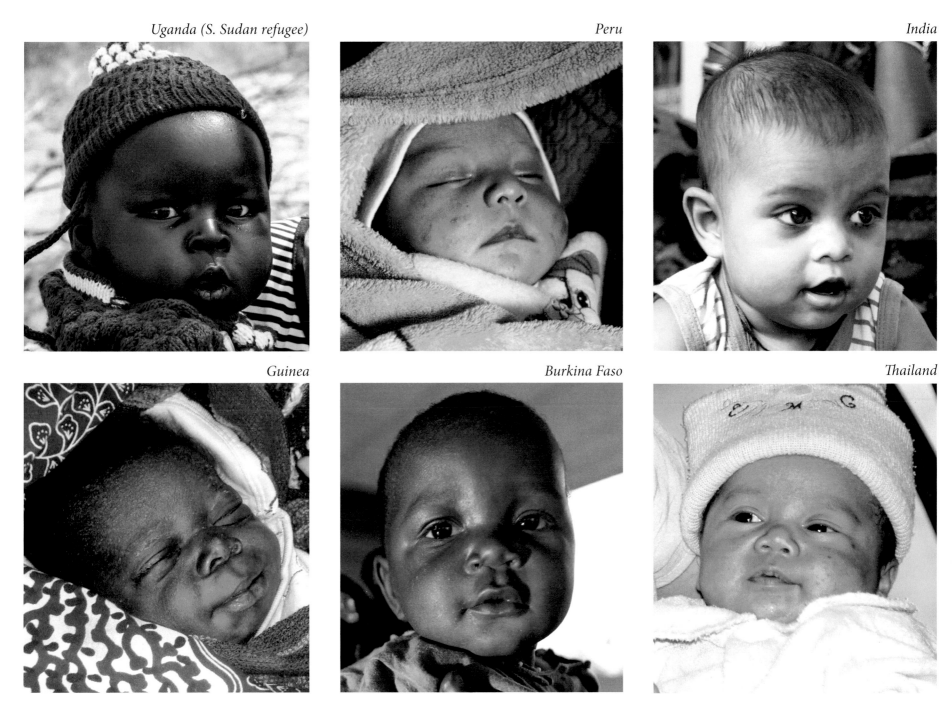

Uganda (S. Sudan refugee) *Peru* *India*

Guinea *Burkina Faso* *Thailand*

It's simply a matter of chance.

As a boy, I will have choices from the day I am born.
Some will be made for me...

Haiti

and some I will make for myself.

Egypt

As a boy, I will be told to be a man,
to work, to fight, to be brave.

South Sudan

But as I am *just* a boy, sometimes I will be afraid.

Benin

As a boy, there will be times when I am very lucky.

I will be able to go to school and learn each day…

Nepal

while my sisters must work

Liberia

and wish for an education…because they are "*just*" girls.

Yet, as a boy, I am also a son and a brother.

El Salvador

One day I might even be a father.

Bangladesh

I want my mother…

my sister…

Nepal

my daughters…

Bangladesh

all children to be free to choose what they want to be.

Indonesia

Because I love her…

I want my sister at school with me.

Ethiopia

Because *I* have a voice…

I will want my daughter's voice heard.

Ireland

I want people to see that we all have voices and choices.

Guatemala

As boys, we can stand up for everyone.

As a boy, I know this is right.

Library and Archives Canada Cataloguing in Publication

As a boy / by Plan International.

Issued in print and electronic formats.
ISBN 978-1-77260-016-2 (hardback).
—ISBN 978-1-77260-017-9 (epub)

1. Boys—Juvenile literature. 2. Boys—Pictorial works.
I. Plan (Organization), author

HQ775.B43 2016   305.230811   C2016-902920-4

C2016-902921-2

Copyright © 2016 Plan International Canada Inc.

*Second Story Press gratefully acknowledges the support of the
Ontario Arts Council and the Canada Council for the Arts for our
publishing program. We acknowledge the financial support of
the Government of Canada through the Canada Book Fund.*

Printed and bound in China

ONTARIO ARTS COUNCIL
CONSEIL DES ARTS DE L'ONTARIO
an Ontario government agency
un organisme du gouvernement de l'Ontario

Canada Council   Conseil des Arts
for the Arts   du Canada

Funded by the Government of Canada
Financé par le gouvernement du Canada | Canada

Published by
Second Story Press
20 Maud Street, Suite 401
Toronto, Ontario, Canada
M5V 2M5
www.secondstorypress.ca

Photo Credits

Cover: James Stone/Plan
Back cover: Richard Wainwright/Plan,
Miguel Vargas Corzantes/Plan, Peter de
Ruiter/Plan, Floor Catshoek/Plan
Title page: Pieter ten Hoopen/Plan
Page 2: (top, L-R) Mortuza Sheikh/
Plan, Claire Grigaut/Plan, Shona
Hamilton/Plan (bottom, L-R) Nandini
Shahla Chowdhury/Plan, Miguel Vargas
Corzantes/Plan, Guido Dingemans/Plan
Page 3: (top, L-R) Rose Sjölander/Plan,
Martha Adams/Girl Rising © 2014,
Floor Catshoek/Plan (bottom, L-R) Aly
Abadara Bangoura/Plan, Alf Berg/Plan,
Cesar Bazan/Plan
Page 4: Shona Hamilton/Plan
Page 5: Katie Dimmer/Plan
Page 6: Luca Tommasini/Plan
Page 7: Nyani Quarmyne/Plan
Page 8: Ollivier Girard/Plan
Page 9: Hatai Limprayoonyong/Plan
Page 10: Peter de Ruiter/Plan
Page 11: Alf Berg/Plan
Page 12: Kaung Htet/Plan
Page 13: Shona Hamilton/Plan
Page 14: Safiul Azam/Plan
Page 15: Alf Berg/Plan
Page 16: Peter de Ruiter/Plan
Page 17: Saikat Mojumder/Plan
Page 18: Floor Catshoek/Plan
Page 19: Peter de Ruiter/Plan
Page 20: Richard Wainwright/Plan
Page 21: Seiha Tiep/Plan
Page 22: Jason Clarke/Plan
Page 23: Miguel Vargas Corzantes/Plan
Page 24: Minttu-Maaria Partanen/Plan